Praise for
*Real Talk?*

"Dr. Croom offers the answer to how to have the deep and honest discussions of race and politics in any of today's classrooms. Politics are embedded and addressed head-on marvelously because of experiences and the learning he has endured. It's a journey well captured for our benefit, even for those on the fence regarding whether they are truly ready. Students are ready to have these conversations. Teachers are ready to lead and ensure it happens. With this clear and concise guide it is now possible."
—Ms. NaShonda L. Bender-Cooke, NBCT, M.Ed.
North Carolina Governor's Teacher Advisory Council Vice-Chair

"*Real Talk? How to Discuss Race, Racism, and Politics in 21st Century American Schools* offers compelling guidance on how to design discussions that are critical to our democracy today and have been across our history. The guidelines and illustrations are revealing for talk within classrooms as well as talk among key stakeholders around schooling. The breadth of Dr. Croom's argument is consequential because it encompasses knowledge, dispositions and epistemological orientations that are necessary for rationale and open debate around complex issues for which there are not simple responses. The discussion has depth as it includes examples that are timely and complex. It is a required read for not only educators, but all those with a stake in how our educational system prepares our young people for civic engagement."

—Dr. Carol D. Lee
Edwina S. Tarry Professor Emerita
Northwestern University

"Given that Covid-19, racial, and political tensions continue to shape our communities and rapidly changing world, *Real Talk?* is a timely and engaging book that provides educators, administrators, and educational stakeholders with practical steps to engage in necessary and meaningful conversations."

—Dr. Stephanie Power-Carter
Professor
The Ohio State University

"*Real Talk?* is an excellent tool for teachers who want to address issues of race in the classroom without running afoul of legislators and others who fear the teaching of race in America's schools. Dr. Croom begins to move us beyond theory toward a practice that is sound, evidence-based and accessible to educators from a wide range of traditions."

—Dr. Marvin Lynn,
Professor
Portland State University

"Written in language that is accessible to a wide range of audiences, this book is essential reading for anyone interested in diversity, equity, and inclusivity, especially in relation to racial justice. Drawing on trenchant insights from W.E.B. Du Bois, James Baldwin, and others, Dr. Croom makes compelling arguments for why redefining "race" more realistically and moving toward increased racial justice in the United States is important, especially given the mutually constitutive relations between public schools and society. Pivotal in these arguments is the claim that race is "consequential social practice," a powerful new way to think about race and racism developed by the author that, alone, is worth reading about. Finally, besides being conceptually sophisticated about the topic it addresses, this book is eminently practical and includes, among other things, references and links to many useful resources, a step-by-step protocol for putting *Real Talk?* into action, and multiple examples of questions and strategies to use to discuss controversial "public issues with credibility, criticality, and confidence."

—Dr. George Kamberelis
Professor, Chair, Graduate Program Director
Department of Education
Western Colorado University

"At a time of reckoning over race and racism—Marcus Croom provides educators with a practical, grounded approach to beginning the dialogue in schools and classrooms. Let the "real talk" begin and flourish with bravery, urgency and force."

—Dr. Allan Luke
Emeritus Professor
Queensland University of Technology, Australia

# Real Talk?

## How to Discuss Race, Racism, and Politics in 21st Century American Schools

MARCUS CROOM, PH.D.

Copyright © 2021 by Marcus Croom

All rights reserved. No part of this book may be reproduced, scanned, or distributed in any printed or electronic form without permission.

Published in the United States of America by Brio Education Consulting, LLC.

Names: Croom, Marcus., 1977- author.
Title: Real talk? / Marcus Croom
Description: First Edition | Indianapolis: Brio Education Consulting, LLC, [2021]
Identifiers: LCCN 2021915293 (print) | LCCN 2021915423 (ebook) | ISBN 978-1-7376787-0-0 (paperback) | ISBN 978-1-7376787-1-7 (ebook)

briolearning.com

First Print Edition: September 2021

# DEDICATION

*Racial literacies and post-White futures for us all.*

# CONTENTS

|   | | |
|---|---|---|
|   | Introduction | i |
| 1 | Why? | 1 |
| 2 | How? | 8 |
| 3 | Real World? | 34 |
| 4 | Conclusion | 46 |
| 5 | Sources | 57 |

## ACKNOWLEDGMENTS

In our feverish times, I hold my loved ones and supporters even closer. Each of you know that you belong here in a grand list where the world can see who has loved and supported me toward this first edition. Thank you for everything, especially understanding.

# INTRODUCTION

*The function of the university is not simply to teach bread-winning, or to furnish teachers for the public schools, or to be a centre of polite society; it is, above all, to be the organ of that fine adjustment between real life and the growing knowledge of life, an adjustment which forms the secret of civilization.*

—Dr. W.E.B. Du Bois, 1903

*Either the United States will destroy ignorance or ignorance will destroy the United States.*

—Dr. W.E.B. Du Bois, 1906

Are we going to have a real talk? There are certainly many reasons why you might decide not to whether you're racially White, Black, Brown, or multiracial. Just look around. Have you noticed that race, racism, and politics have been crescendoing in American society and schools? For example, critical race theory (CRT) is literally being banned in some American schools—despite the fact that CRT is widely unknown and much less likely taught in American schools; headlines repeatedly report stories of teachers epically failing in their attempts to teach about American enslavement and racism; social media circulates cringey clips of student-recorded moments from inside American classrooms; racially White parents are going viral and gaining some support as they voice outrage and pain at the idea of White fragility, White privilege, and White supremacy in the United States of America; facts and alternative facts seem to be equivalent for some in American politics, news, and society; even Dr. Seuss' books and Hasbro's Potato Head toys have been held up in some political circles as symbols of a grave culture war; and on and on. So, are we going to have a real talk? A real talk in schools about public issues like race, racism, and politics?

In this book, here's what I mean by **"real talk"**: a reality-based talk, an evidence-based talk, or even an empirically supported talk about public issues at school in the United States of America (or elsewhere). "Real talk" also means: authentic dialogue (Du Bois, 1923), a true word (Freire, 1970), liberating uses of language (Hurston, 2018), or just sayin' what nee-da-be said, using any number of languages and lingos, in order to tell it like it is about public issues at school in the United States of America.

Additionally, **race** is defined as *consequential social practice* in this book. In other words, throughout this book race is not understood according to the common sense view that most readers would expect and assume. Instead, race is understood as something human beings *think and do for good or ill*. Race is human practice, not a natural or biological actuality. For more about practice of race theory (PRT), read this [research](#).

In alignment with PRT, **racism** is a form of thinking or doing race for ill—individually, with others, or institutionally—such as disrespecting, disregarding, distorting, deceiving, or degrading human beings. According to this definition, most readers could offer some examples of racism if asked to share. In the United States of America, racism has often been practiced in a manner that benefited those regarded as racially White. For a few examples of racism, take a look at this evidence.

The final focal term of this book title—**politics**—means conflicting efforts to (re)distribute various forms of capital (social, cultural, political, financial, etc.), all of which are valued by human beings to some degree. Such politics may be ethical or unethical, helpful or harmful, explicit or implied, and effective or ineffective. For a brief look at American politics, watch this lesson on American Government.

Who is asked to have these real talks? School educators (administrators, teachers, specialists, coaches, etc.) with the support of legislators, school board members, parents, community educators, college educators, education journalists, and other societal stakeholders. In this book, school educators are not imagined as neutral, pristine professionals who merely carry out their schooling functions. It is precisely as environmentally, culturally, linguistically, socially, racially, economically, and politically interested human beings that I ask school educators to commit themselves to the practices involved with having a real talk. Likewise, each school student who participates in a real talk should be regarded as having their own particular assets and interests as human beings in community with peers or adults. Later, I will explain why these kinds of discussions are necessary in 21st century American schools, but here it is important to share a little about myself in this regard and then mention a major assumption of this guide.

Who is asking school educators to have a real talk? Who has authored this first edition, what embeds this human being, and what has produced this writer—to some degree—in 2021? In 2017, I wrote the opening episode of a [micro-comparative memoir](#) in order to answer a related question about myself. In 2021, this book has become the unforeseen occasion to add the next installment of this ongoing memoir.

**Click**: Facebook post, January 6, 2021
https://www.facebook.com/iammarcuscroom/posts/74046 7139909867

Available here is a high-definition version of David W. Griffith's complete 1915 film, *The Birth of a Nation*.

**Click**: Black Lives Matter in Literacy Research Panel, December 3, 2020; Annual Meeting of the Literacy Research Association (LRA) | 2020 Video Excerpt | 2021 Publication

As the snapshots above begin to show, I wrote this book out of my experiences as a cisgender male, straight, Black, low-income-rooted and upwardly mobile, race critical researcher from Goldsboro, NC (Southeastern U.S.A.) with undergraduate and graduate degrees from Historically Black Colleges and Universities (HBCUs). Born during the late 1970s, my life includes (nonunionized) K-12 teaching and leadership experiences as a Music Educator in North Carolina, as well as Black Christian laity and ministry experiences ranging from New First Corinthian United Holy Church (Dudley, NC) to Trinity United Church of Christ (Chicago, IL). As an [awarded faculty member](#) at Indiana University Bloomington with an earned Ph.D. in Curriculum and Instruction from University of Illinois at Chicago, I have carefully examined American society and schooling from many professional and personal angles. For instance, my unpaid and paid service work includes Illinois [nonprofits](#), North Carolina & Illinois schools and school districts, [University of Chicago Urban Labs](#), and [University of Louisville](#). This 2021 book is, to varying degrees, a product of all of this and more (e.g. life as a son, sibling, uncle, husband, father, and so on). More specifically, I wrote this book in response to indirect and [direct](#) evidence that school educators in the U.S.A. desired some support with discussing public issues like race, racism, and politics in 21st century American schools.

This book is written to the broad audience listed above with the major assumption that school educators have already established their own standing and understanding as credible conversationalists in their school. For example, if a school educator is generally not perceived as credible by children and adults in discussions of public issues like race, racism, and politics this would suggest that the school educator's own standing and understanding related to these kinds of discussions has not already been established. As such, the school educator would first develop their own standing and understanding as a credible conversationalist in their school, then begin to carry out the five-step, real talk protocol© offered in this book. In other words, real talks are launched from the real standing and understanding of <u>credible conversationalists</u> (also see "Pre-launch &

Learn" in Chapter 2). To explore ways to establish the kind of standing and understanding that discussions of race, racism, and politics demand these days, check out the scholarship, consulting, and professional development offered by Dr. Marcus Croom. Also, stay tuned to this *Classroom to Community Support Series* from Brio Education Consulting, LLC.

Since each one of us is an accountable participant of society, and even of our schools: Are *you* going to have a real talk?

If you are undecided, read on. If you've already decided to have a real talk at your school, jump to Chapter 2 "How?" and move forward. After your real talk, let me know how it went: Join our mailing list to receive an invitation to our private Facebook group community.

# Real Talk?

# 1 WHY?

Why is it necessary to have teacher- or administrator-student discussions about public issues like race, racism, and politics in the 21st century? Because all of these are already playing out in our national and international public life and likewise in our schools across the United States of America. This means that from preschool to post-graduate schooling, countries and communities impact classrooms. For example, we typically think of curricula as something that comes from schools. However, few realize that school curricula routinely reflect what is valued, or even simply what is popular, in society—whether what is valued or popular is true or false. Here's how Dr. W. E. Burghardt Du Bois documented this insight over 100 years ago in the United States of America:

> *This theory of human culture* [that is, thinking that "human culture" means universally modern, racially White, and excusably exploitative] *and its aims has worked itself through warp and woof* [that is, constitutes the fabric] *of **our daily thought with a thoroughness that few realize**. Everything great, good, efficient, fair, and honorable is "white"; everything mean, bad, blundering, cheating, and dishonorable is "yellow"; a bad taste is "brown"; and the devil is "black." The changes of this theme are continually rung

> *in picture and story, in newspaper heading and moving-picture, in sermon and* **school book**, *until, of course, the King can do no wrong,—a White Man is always right and a Black Man has no rights which a white man is bound to respect.* (Darkwater, 1920, p. 44)

In other words, human-designed societies and communities have always impacted human-designed schools and classrooms, just as classrooms and schools impact communities and societies, whether such influence is acknowledged or unacknowledged. School educators who are asked to provide some warrant or justification for having a real talk should highlight these interrelations among human-designed society and schooling as well as the *reality imperative* that results. The reality imperative is constituted by **demands for society and schools to have a contested degree of congruence and relevance** to one another, amid **competing human differences,**

**desires, and designs.** Therefore, the reason why school educators should have a real talk in school is because of the imperative produced by interinfluence with the real world. *Real talks are a response to the reality imperative of living and learning in the real world.* Figure 1 is a diagram of the reality imperative.

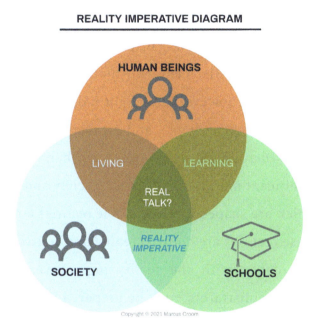

**Figure 1: Diagram of the Reality Imperative**

Although this first edition of *Real Talk?* is not intended to enumerate them, there are many examples and citations that could elaborate or illustrate the interinfluences of society and schools as well as the reality imperative (Lane, 1932; Thompson, 1934; Baldwin, 1963). For our purposes here, the point is that the foundational relationship between human-designed society and schools is the reason why real talks, instead of unreal talks, are necessary in 21st century American schools. This means that however one might judge the quality of our society or schools, and no matter the impacts these may have upon one another, there are significant mutualities between society and schools, which are shaped by inescapable realities (and often these realities are human created and controlled). In accordance with the reality imperative, teachers and administrators must be prepared to respond to and/or initiate discussions about these realities that occur beyond and within schools. *Real lives, in the real world, require real talk in school.*

But what about professional neutrality about controversial issues? In this book, non-partisan is not the same as non-factual or non-personal. We are all living in our world, and in some nation, which means our personal and professional lives are already affected by controversies and competing claims. The aim of this guide is to support good faith discussions about public issues—like race, racism, and politics—based on credible information that anyone can access. My hope is that across the political spectrum and whatever one's personal or professional interests may be, the readers of this book have committed themselves to veracity. Assuming that your aim is to have truthful discussions of public issues in school, we now turn to how you can have a real talk.

## 2 HOW?

The real talk protocol© is designed both to illuminate opportunities to discuss public issues—like race, racism, and politics—and to inform those who have this critical discussion. As a transparent interrogation framework, the real talk process is introduced below without specifying a public issue, topic, or focus of discussion. I present the real talk guidelines without offering a particular issue in order to emphasize the five-step process rather than how it might work in a particular discussion. My intention is to invite readers to have a panoramic view of the public issue discussions that might be initiated and informed by a real talk.

Although there are many moving parts involved in this five-step process, the point of using the real talk protocol is to have an honest, probing, constructive conversation about controversial public issues in school. To accomplish this result, you will need to *plan* and *preview* the discussion you choose to have before you launch. Once you launch a discussion, you will *put in context* whatever you converse about as you *point out evidence* related to that public issue during your real talk. According to your plan, you will conclude the discussion at some point, whether or not the public issue(s) discussed have been resolved among the participants. Because real talks are intended for discussion of controversial public issues in schools, many of which will not be resolved by the discussions you launch, you will expect to thoughtfully *pin up & return* to unresolved discussions (and even those discussions that seem resolved but really are not). For example, your real talk cannot resolve the current (mis)characterizations of critical race theory (CRT) in American politics and education, so this public issue is well-suited for school educators to *pin up & return* as this raging controversy continues to unfold. As a different example, a real talk could resolve questions about why some Dr. Suess books will no longer be published or why the Hasbro company elected to rename their Potato Head toys (both have published answers on their websites; see links in [Introduction](Introduction)). Yet, changes in participant or public sentiment may become reason enough to *return* to any public issue. Furthermore, in any discussion there are unvoiced items, misunderstood items, and unintended items. All of these items are additional reasons to *return* to your real talk. Whatever the case, to *return* to your previously selected and launched discussion you will need to note any insights that you can draw from your previous real talk. These insights will be useful as you *plan* and *preview* your next real talk...which you will then launch, *put in context, point out evidence, pin up & return,* and so on. Figure 2 illustrates the five-step, real talk protocol (RTP)©.

**Figure 2: Diagram of the Real Talk Protocol (RTP)©**

**Episode 1: Pre-Launch & Learn**

This five-step protocol has two episodes, *pre-launch* and *launch*. For intended results, this protocol should be followed as designed with the understanding that contexts differ. During both episodes school educators are learning, unlearning, and relearning to advance themselves as professionals and as human beings. The first two steps of this real talk protocol—Plan and Preview—comprise the *pre-launch episode* and the final three steps—Put In Context, Point Out Evidence, Pin Up & Return—comprise the *launch episode*.

***RTP Step 1: Plan*** *Discussion(s)*

You should plan your discussion before any real talk is launched. Within this planning step, there are at least four areas to include in your plan: *general details, meaning details, material details,* and *maintenance details.*

*General details* answer basic questions about the real talk you will have such as: the public issue(s) you have chosen, who will be included in your discussion, and when you will have your discussion. These general details will also clarify the structure, setting, and duration of your real talk, including the stopping point of a single discussion and the sequence and schedule of multiple discussions.

*Meaning details* involve questions about the written and unwritten (mis)understandings of the public issue(s) you have chosen. This area of your plan requires you to notice various meaningful representations involved with the public issue you will discuss. For example, there may be videos, billboards, stickers, texts, shirts, speeches, websites, films, events, and so on that shed light on how individuals, groups, or institutions are (mis)understanding the public issue you have selected. Here it is important to identify multiple views of the public issue(s) you have selected, whether these views have changed over time, and the benefits of getting a reliable understanding of that public issue.

*Material details* will require you to examine the way resources are (not) currently or have (not) historically been distributed from the standpoint of place, power, prestige, position, purpose, posterity, and so on. In other words, this area of your plan 'follows the money' so to speak related to your public issue(s) and the impact that this money has in the real world. The planning questions raised here will likely highlight some insightful connections between race, racism, and politics in the United States of America and globally.

*Maintenance details* bring to light some of the actors, aims, apparatuses, and associations that (re)create public issues. Importantly, this area of planning involves bringing forward the voices of institutions, leaders, groups, lobbies, political parties, and so on, as they speak of themselves in comparison to reliable records of their own practices.

All four of these planning areas should be used both to interrogate the selected public issue(s) and the person(s) who will carry out the real talk. Planning characterizes all real talks.

To guide practitioners through this first step of the real talk protocol, I have provided a [free template](#) with questions to consider. Additionally, below are at least four areas that should interrogate and inform your real talk before you launch a discussion. The free template provided and the tables below are not comprehensive, and both will be revised in future editions of *Real Talk?*

### General: The Basics of Discussing Public Issues

-What public issue(s) will be discussed in this real talk?
-Who will be included in this real talk?
-What needs to be said in this real talk and what does not?
-How will you say what needs to be said in this real talk?
-When will you have this real talk and why at that moment?
-What is the point of having this real talk with these persons? (for example, awareness? authoring? action?)
-How will you conclude this real talk? How will you return to it? And when?
-Who are the individuals and/or disaggregated and aggregated groups involved with the public issue(s) discussed in this real talk? How is their humanity (dis)respected?
-Lesson, unit, event?
-Team or individual real talk?
-Face-to-face, virtual, hybrid?

### Meaning: The (Mis)Understandings of Public Issues

-What visual(s), language(s), narrative(s) and/or counternarrative(s) are involved with the public issue(s) that will be discussed in this real talk?
-What views have (not) changed about the public issue(s) that will be discussed in this real talk? And why?
-Who individually or collectively benefits from (mis)understanding the public issue(s) that will be discussed in this real talk? And how?

### Material: The (Mal)Distributed Resources of Public Issues

-How is money, business, and/or ownership involved with the public issue(s) that will be discussed in this real talk? And how is support or opposition related to this public issue funded?
-Which place(s) and/or ordinance zone(s) are involved with the public issue(s) that will be discussed in this real talk?
-What is the impact of the public issue(s) among those below the median income? At the median income? Above the median income? And what is important about the relative and absolute differences between these income groups?
-Is there evidence that the public issue(s) that will be discussed in this real talk involve insecurity, loss, inequality, solidarity, or upward mobility? And for whom?

### Maintenance: The (Re)Construction of Public Issues

-What institutions and ideologies are involved with the public issue(s) that will be discussed in this real talk?
-Who are the leaders involved with the public issue(s) discussed in this real talk?
-Which interest group(s), lobbies, and/or political parties are involved with the public issue(s) that will be discussed in this real talk? What are the competing and the complementary views of those group(s), lobbyist(s) and/or parties? And what do those group(s), lobbyist(s) and/or parties say they are for? Compared to what those group(s) and/or parties have said they are for, what do records show that they have done thus far?
-How have enabling or blocking coalitions shaped the public issue(s) discussed in this real talk?

**RTP Step 2: Preview** *Discussion(s) with Others*

You should also preview your discussion before any real talk is launched. Who might be willing to preview your real talk? The possibilities are endless, but here are at least five sensible options:
- Teachers and/or administrators?
- Experts? (persons with mastery of research or experience)
- Parents or guardians?
- Community groups or organizations?
- Other school or societal stakeholders?

The purpose of step 2 is to clearly communicate the details of your upcoming real talk and refine the structure, setting, and duration of your real talk, including the stopping point of a single discussion and the sequence and schedule of multiple discussions (see RTP Step 1). Additionally, this step creates opportunities for school educators to provide warrants for and to lock-in support for the upcoming real talk, whether verbally or in writing. All real talks are designed to constructively address controversial, difficult, and even "hot-button" public issues critically, so practitioners should expect resistance, deflection, or even forms of aggression during this step. The point is to work through these typical forms of resistance for the higher mission of *cultivating more human fulfillment and mitigating human suffering* in schools and society. This should go without saying, but to be abundantly clear: the school educator who is planning, previewing, and launching a real talk is part of the solution with regard to public issues like race, racism, and politics. In contrast, unreal talks, avoidance, and silence are part of the problem in American society and schooling (see figure 1).

To increase the likelihood that step 2 will result in launching your real talk, I recommend the following:

- Engage the formal and informal power structure(s) of your school and openly document each exchange related to your real talk (trust and verify).

-Avoid all forms of isolation, disconnection, and unresponsiveness as you preview your real talk (keep following up!)

-Invite and announce "buy-in" without allowing the lack of unanimous support to hinder the real talk protocol© process (early supporters can generate broader support).

-Build authentic community around practicing real talks in your school (leverage supportive relationships with various internal and external school stakeholders).

Future editions of *Real Talk?* will include additional tools and strategies designed to support practitioners as they navigate and complete this crucial preview step of the real talk protocol©. Join the Brio Education Consulting, LLC [mailing list](mailing list) for updates.

## Episode 2: Launch & Learn

After completing the pre-launch episode, school educators launch a real talk. As mentioned, the final three steps of the real talk protocol© comprise the launch episode.

*RTP Step 3: Put In Context for Discussion(s)*

You should launch any real talk according to effective teaching and learning practices. For example: (1) prepare the spacial and social atmosphere beforehand; (2) prepare the materials you will use before you launch; (3) pleasantly invite the attention of discussion participants to begin your real talk; (4) clearly state the issue, aim, and activities of the discussion; (5) establish the norms of exchange for the conversation; and (6) follow the plan you have created for your real talk with sensitivity to "teachable moments" or the necessity to reasonably change your plan as you learn during the launch episode.

Croom

As mentioned at the start of this chapter, I have not specified which real talks should occur in schools to invite readers to approach the real talk protocol© with a panoramic view of the public issues that could be discussed. Accordingly, the following are suggestions for how school educators might frame and put into context any discussion selected for a real talk:

-Describe the historical, national, local, curricular, and other *staging* within which your chosen public issue is occurring.
-Frame your public issue with at least 20 prior years; even if you don't share all of the details you know about your 20 year *timeline*, you should be familiar with relevant details from those preceding years before you have a real talk in school (see [RTP Step 1](RTP Step 1)); refer to this timeline during your selected discussion.
-Why 20+ years? We all have the tendency to view human history and events from the

reference point of our birth. By using at least a 20 year time frame, this broadens the point of reference for school-aged learners (and even adults) during the discussion of your public issue. Think of *stating your frame* like this: "Before you were born, this issue was already in progress and here's what was going on...." In cases where the selected public issue was not occurring 20 years prior, report the origins of your chosen public issue and share the appropriate time frame.

There are countless sources that might be used to inform or present the staging, timeline, and framing of public issues. Following are some examples related to race, racism, and politics in the United States of America:

*Online Examples*
Elementary and Secondary Education Act(s) (ESEA) 1965-2015

https://oese.ed.gov/offices/office-of-administration/about-us/legislation/

Racism is a Public Health Crisis
https://www.apha.org/Topics-and-Issues/Health-Equity/Racism-and-health/Racism-Declarations

The Roots of Structural Racism Project
https://belonging.berkeley.edu/roots-structural-racism

The Opportunity Atlas
https://www.opportunityatlas.org/

Gallop Center on Black Voices
https://news.gallup.com/315575/measuring-black-voices.aspx

Inquire Indiana: What's the History of Racism in Indiana? https://youtu.be/v8eAHpl3dUQ

Use of Racial Terms in 19th Century Literature
https://www.c-span.org/video/?302493-1/racial-terms-19th-century-literature

King in the Wilderness
https://www.hbo.com/documentaries/king-in-the-wilderness

The Soul of America
https://www.hbo.com/documentaries/the-soul-of-america

The Neutral Ground
https://www.pbs.org/pov/watch/neutralground/video-the-neutral-ground/

James G. Johnson's letter: "Should I Sacrifice to Live 'Half-American?'"
https://www.newspapers.com/clip/33240765/james-g-thompsons-letter-to-the/

*Print & Digital Examples*

Bacon's Rebellion in 1676 according to Ira Berlin

**1790 U.S. Naturalization Act**

Theodore Dwight Weld (1839): *American Slavery As It Is*

Frederick Douglass (1845): *Narrative of the Life of Frederick Douglass, An American Slave*

Harriet Jacobs (1861): *Incidents in the Life of a Slave Girl*

George Washington Williams (1882; 1887): *A History of the Negro Race in America from 1619 to 1880; Negroes as Slaves, as Soldiers, and as Citizens, Vol. 1 &2* and *A History of Negro Troops in the War of the Rebellion*

**1894 founding of the <ins>United Daughters of the Confederacy</ins> (UDC) & 1896 founding of the <ins>National Association of Colored Women's Clubs</ins> (NACWC); also 1896** *<ins>Plessy v. Ferguson</ins>* **U.S. Supreme Court Decision**

W. E. Burghardt Du Bois (1935): *Black Reconstruction in America, 1860-1880*

Rayford W. Logan (1944): *What the Negro Wants*

**1952 U.S. Immigration and Nationality Act**

Rayford W. Logan (1954, 1965): *The Betrayal of the Negro: From Rutherford B. Hayes to Woodrow Wilson*; **also 1954** <ins>*Brown vs. Board of Education*</ins> **U.S. Supreme Court Decision**

Alex Haley & Malcolm X (1964): *The Autobiography of Malcolm X*

Kevin Phillips (1969, 2015): *The Emerging Republican Majority*

John Hope Franklin (1991): *Race and History*

Patricia Reid-Merritt (2018): *A State-by-State History of Race and Racism in the United States ([Vol. 1-2](#))*

Middleton A. Harris, Morris Levitt, Roger Furman & Ernest Smith (2019): *The Black Book*

**2021 U.S. Citizenship Act**

[https://www.whitehouse.gov/briefing-room/statements-releases/2021/01/20/fact-sheet-president-biden-sends-immigration-bill-to-congress-as-part-of-his-commitment-to-modernize-our-immigration-system/](https://www.whitehouse.gov/briefing-room/statements-releases/2021/01/20/fact-sheet-president-biden-sends-immigration-bill-to-congress-as-part-of-his-commitment-to-modernize-our-immigration-system/)

Other books on history: Robinson ([1997](#)), Klinkner & Smith ([2002](#)), Mann ([2005](#)), Zinn ([2005](#)), Painter ([2006](#)), Loewen ([2007](#)), Pinder ([2013](#)), Dunbar-Ortiz ([2015](#)), Baptist ([2016](#)), Kendi ([2016](#)), Isenberg ([2017](#)), Rothstein ([2017](#)), Hurston ([2018](#)), Ortiz ([2018](#)), Berry & Gross ([2020](#)), Pinder ([2020](#)), etc.

Other books on religion and politics: Kimball (2008), Lambert (2010), Cone (2011), Wald & Calhoun-Brown (2018), etc.

The resources listed above are provided as an incomplete, exploratory illustration of how doable it is to learn about and share at least 20 years of the staging, timeline, and framing of public issues like race, racism, and politics. There are numerous additional sources that school educators could consult to inform the pre-launch and launch episodes of a real talk.

***RTP Step 4: Point Out*** *Evidence Base During Discussion(s)*

Personal experiences should be valued and shared in both the pre-launch and launch episodes, but a real talk includes evidence beyond one's personal experience. There are many available sources to turn to for evidence in the 21st century, some more reliable than others. Here's the point of step 4: What reliable, publicly available information will anchor your discussion(s)? Most of this evidence should have been gathered during the pre-launch episode (see [RTP Step 1 & 2](#)) so that now, during the launch episode, the focus is on sharing this evidence during the real talk. Just as you stated your frame in the previous step, think of *stating your facts* like this: "Here are some important facts about this issue...and here is where you can find more...." When it comes to public issues like race, racism, and politics there is an abundance of credible knowledge to draw upon (for example, Raoul Peck's [film](#) and [essential reading & viewing](#) lists offer easily accessible evidence from human history). Among numerous things that might be used to point out evidence during a real talk, here are a few possibilities:

    -primary sources?
    -news?
    -interviews?
    -images?

-maps?

-recordings?

-fiction or nonfiction texts?

-films or plays?

-other credible documentation?

To offer just one example that combines "news" and "interviews" to point out evidence, I mention here an exclusive news article from *The Nation* and a 1981 interview of Lee Atwater. In this instance, "news" and "interviews" are pointing out evidence of dog whistle politics in American society. Many more single or combined possibilities from above might be used to point out evidence during a real talk.

**RTP Step 5: Pin Up** Inconclusiveness **& Thoughtfully Return** to Discussion(s)

As explained in RTP Step 3, the origins of many public issues—especially race, racism, and politics—predate the lives of real talk participants.

*Real Talk?*

How realistic is it, then, to expect that a single discussion or even a series of discussions will resolve the issue at hand? Such a false expectation would result in an unreal talk instead of a real talk. With the **reality imperative** in full view (see [figure 1](#)), think of *stating your finale* like this: "As we said earlier, this issue was already in progress before you were born so we are closing this discussion, but we are not finished with this issue." If you have planned a series of discussions (see [Episode 1: Pre-launch & Learn](#)), add to this finale statement a preview of what will be discussed next. Also, highlight the issue, aim, and activities of this discussion again and assess the outcomes of your planning. For instance, revisit this question from the "[The Basics of Discussing Public Issues](#)" table above: *What is the point of having this real talk with these persons (for example, awareness? authoring? action?).* Whether you have planned a single discussion or a series of discussions, close by acknowledging inconclusiveness and designating a

31

follow up occasion that reviews the previous discussion and updates the previous discussion (updates such as, new evidence, closer examination, shifts in participant understanding or view, relevant current events, and so on). Overall, this final step requires school educators to respond thoughtfully to considerations like the following at the very least:

-What will likely be unresolved by the end of this real talk? In other words, fully expect for good discussions to come to an end without resolve. *Prepare the end before you begin* (see [Episode 1: Pre-launch and Learn](#)).

-Across RTP Step 2, 3 & 5 set appropriate expectations when offering warrants for your real talk: *Ending a discussion is not the same as resolving a public issue.*

-Revisit and assess outcomes for: "What is the point of having this real talk with these persons (for example, awareness? authoring? action?)" *A real talk advances learning.*

-When real talk participants come back for more, actually provide more.

As shown at the beginning of this chapter, a planned *return* to a previously selected and launched discussion requires that school educators note any insights that can be drawn from previous real talks and use these insights to *plan* and *preview* an upcoming real talk (see [figure 2](#)).

The real talk protocol© adds to a wide range of ongoing work that responds to the reality imperative of 21st century society and schools in the United States of America (see [figure 1](#)). If useful, broader implementation of the real talk protocol© is welcomed for additional domains (society and *x*) and additional national contexts.

# 3 REAL WORLD?

Chapter 1 provides explicit warrant for a real talk in American schools. Chapter 2 provides a detailed explanation of how to have a real talk in American schools. This chapter uses an example of new state legislation to offer a glimpse of the real talk protocol© in the real world.

Of all of the chapters in this book, this one may be the most challenging for some readers to digest.

## Real Talk?

If this chapter is not as easy-to-read as I intend, please know that it's not because of you. Here's why this chapter might be less accessible for some readers: I'm engaging legislative lingo, complex and competing sociopolitical agendas, countercultural notions of race, and more all in one chapter of a short read book. So why include this chapter at all, right? Because I owe my readers a glimpse of how the real talk protocol© works in the real world—beyond the neat margins of this book. In this chapter, I focus on state legislation because I see it as the most useful real world demo. Even if some readers are working outside of the state I have selected for this demo, it is possible that other American states might pursue similar state legislation. My hope is that school educators working in local schools will benefit from thinking through a state level example of real world legislation as they adopt the real talk protocol© in their schools. So, aware of the risk of confusing some readers, here goes my first attempt at placing

35

the real talk protocol© into the context of our real world in 2021.

Using Tennessee's "Conference Committee Report on House Bill No. 580/Senate Bill No. 623," readers will have the opportunity to begin to judge for themselves whether or not the real talk protocol© is suitable for various state education contexts in 2021 and beyond. This judgement call is especially pertinent to those living and learning in states that plan to sign legislation similar to Tennessee's regarding public issues like race, racism, and politics. To provide this glimpse, I show Section 51-53 of Tennessee's new law, as reported by their General Assembly, then note the relevant elements of the real talk protocol©, as delineated in this book. The glimpses below are not intended to walk readers through the five-step process covered in the previous chapters. Rather, these glimpses allow real talk practitioners to begin to think through having a real talk within our real world conditions. In case it helps, read this

*Chalkbeat* article about Tennessee's recent education legislation before moving to the next section.

**A Glimpse of the Real Talk Protocol (RTP) in the Real World**

The following shares excerpts from Tennessee's new law and offers two glimpses of how a real talk would unfold under their new legislation.

First excerpt from "Conference Committee Report on House Bill No. 580/Senate Bill No. 623":

SECTION 51. Tennessee Code Annotated, Title 49, Chapter 6, Part 10, is amended by adding the following as a new section:

(a) An LEA or public charter school shall not include or promote the following concepts as part of a course of instruction or in a curriculum or instructional program, or allow teachers or other employees of the LEA or public charter school to use supplemental instructional materials that include or promote the following concepts:

(1) One (1) race or sex is inherently superior to another race or sex;
(2) An individual, by virtue of the individual's race or sex, is inherently privileged, racist, sexist, or oppressive, whether consciously or subconsciously;
(3) An individual should be discriminated against or receive adverse treatment because of the individual's race or sex;
(4) An individual's moral character is determined by the individual's race or sex;
(5) An individual, by virtue of the individual's race or sex, bears responsibility for actions committed in the past by other members of the same race or sex;
(6) An individual should feel discomfort, guilt, anguish, or another form of psychological distress solely because of the individual's race or sex;
(7) A meritocracy is inherently racist or sexist, or designed by a particular race or sex to oppress members of another race or sex;
(8) This state or the United States is fundamentally or irredeemably racist or sexist;
(9) Promoting or advocating the violent overthrow of the United States government;
(10) Promoting division between, or resentment of, a race, sex, religion, creed, nonviolent political affiliation, social class, or class of people;

(11) Ascribing character traits, values, moral or ethical codes, privileges, or beliefs to a race or sex, or to an individual because of the individual's race or sex;
(12) The rule of law does not exist, but instead is a series of power relationships and struggles among racial or other groups;
(13) All Americans are not created equal and are not endowed by their Creator with certain unalienable rights, including, life, liberty, and the pursuit of happiness; or
(14) Governments should deny to any person within the government's jurisdiction the equal protection of the law.

## *Real World Glimpse 1*

The real talk protocol© was designed to be compatible with **practice of race theory (PRT)**. Although it is outside the scope of this first edition to expound at length, PRT allows us to understand race without perpetuating our past and present racial customs in the United States of America (and beyond). Our racial past and present includes debunked ideas about race, such as bodily and biological falsities about human beings. Thus far, our racial customs have also engineered consequential racial hierarchies, despite the fact that *there has never been any basis or justification for the thoughts and practices of White supremacy* (e.g. degradation, discrimination, redlining, segregation, and so on). Importantly, the durability of our racial past and present has contributed to the false (but reasonable!) presumption that race and racism are foreordered and unalterable. Accordingly, a real talk about race, for instance, would define race and discuss race according to the "consequential social practice view," rather than the "common sense view" (Croom, 2020a). To be clear, all forms of race evasion and all postracial views are rejected in PRT. In other words, any real talk about race in school would reject the false biological notion of race, reject the false notion of White supremacy, and critique all forms of racial evasion and racial inevitability (for the origins of the **post-White orientation** see Croom, 2016). When race is understood as *consequential social practice*, our racial past and present need not be our racial future (Croom, 2020b).

However, to correct the harmful ways that race has been practiced—and is currently being practiced—in American society and schools, the institutions, groups, families, and individuals that constitute our society and schools (see figure 1) must *think and do race* in ways that regard the inherent value and undeniable humanity of all in American society and schools (Croom et al., 2021). Here are some common ways that race is practiced in American schools:

- Attributing academic or intellectual capacity to racial classification (such as White = advanced or Black = basic);
- Limiting social-cultural experience to racial classification (such as middle class or blue collar = White); and/or
- Assuming that human bodies self-evidently prove racial classification (such as skin hue = racial classification).

Importantly, anyone may think and do race for good or ill (for example, in meritocratic ways or antimeritocratic ways). Also, anyone can develop multiple literacies through living and learning, including racial literacies (Croom, 2016; Croom, 2020c; www.racialliteracies.org). Furthermore, each one of us is accountable for our own participation in ongoing racialization in the United States of America, racialization which began before any of this book's readers were born (Croom, 2020b; Croom et al., 2019). All of this illustrates that having a real talk about race—as defined in practice of race theory (PRT)—in a Tennessee school would not violate subsection (a) of Section 51 in the state law shown above.

Second excerpt from "Conference Committee Report on House Bill No. 580/Senate Bill No. 623":

(b) Notwithstanding subsection (a), this section does not prohibit an LEA or public charter school from including, as part of a course of instruction or in a curriculum or instructional program, or from allowing teachers or other employees of the LEA or public charter school to use supplemental instructional materials that include:

(1) The history of an ethnic group, as described in textbooks and instructional materials adopted in accordance with part 22 of this chapter;
(2) The impartial discussion of controversial aspects of history;
(3) The impartial instruction on the historical oppression of a particular group of people based on race, ethnicity, class, nationality, religion, or geographic region; or
(4) Historical documents relevant to subdivisions (b)(1) - (3) that are permitted under § 49-6-1011.

## *Real World Glimpse 2*

As I have already stated in the previous chapters of this book, the real talk protocol© is designed to systematically interrogate and inform all participants in their discussions of public issues like race, racism, and politics. If school educators follow the guidelines in Chapter 2, this will include: (1) the "history of an ethnic group" and even the history of "textbooks and instructional materials" used in schools; (2) non-partisan yet factual and inescapably personal "discussion of controversial aspects of history" as well as (3) "instruction on the historical oppression of a particular group of people based on [mostly the common sense view of] race, ethnicity, nationality, religion, or geographic region;" and (4) thorough use of "historical documents relevant to subdivisions (b)(1)-(3)" as shown above. In other words, the real talk protocol© provided in this book would not violate subsection (b) of Section 51 in the state law shown above.

The remaining portions of Tennessee's House Bill No. 580/Senate Bill No. 623 stipulate other aspects of their new law and the following excerpt is shared merely to put these glimpses above in Tennessee's policy context:

(c) If the commissioner of education finds that an LEA or public charter school knowingly violated this section, then the commissioner shall withhold state funds, in an amount determined by the commissioner, from the LEA or public charter school until the LEA or public charter school provides evidence to the commissioner that the LEA or public charter school is no longer in violation of this section.

SECTION 52. If any provision of Section 51 or its application to any person or circumstance is held invalid, then the invalidity does not affect other provisions or applications of Section 51, or of this act, that can be given effect without the invalid provision or application, and to that end, the provisions of this act are severable.

SECTION 53. Section 51 of this act takes effect upon becoming a law, the public welfare requiring it, and applies to the 2021-2022 school year and subsequent school years. All other sections of this act take effect upon becoming a law, the public welfare requiring it.

In summary, the real world demo provided in this chapter is intended to invite readers and real talk practitioners to begin to think through having a real talk beyond this book and within their own state and local contexts.

## 4 CONCLUSION

In short, the five-step real talk protocol© is a systematic way to discuss public issues with credibility, criticality, clarity, and confidence. The real talk process simultaneously questions school educators who will carry out the real talk, generates well-informed planning, and demands veracity throughout. No approach exists which can prevent baseless complaints, false accusations, unethical interferences, or motivated dishonesty from arising in 21st century American schooling. What the real talk protocol© does offer is a transparent interrogation framework that is defensible in various professional contexts—whether the school educator is racially White, Black, Brown, or multiracial.

Chapter 1 provides explicit warrant for a real talk in American schools. That chapter states why school educators should have a real talk in American schools because it is not taken for granted that all readers will see such discussions as necessary. Chapter 2 is a detailed explanation of how to have a real talk in American schools and includes a free template that school educators can use during the pre-launch episode. Notwithstanding the level of guidance provided, chapter 2 is not comprehensive. School educators are advised to commit to ongoing professional development, further reading & listening, practice & process changes, and personal growth after reading this book. Chapter 3 considers an example of new state legislation, offering a glimpse of the real talk protocol© in the real world. The point of this chapter is to begin moving the Real Talk Protocol (RTP)© out toward American society and American schools. Overall, these concise chapters are designed to demonstrate that our current times, even if distressing, demand that school educators respond to the reality imperative, beginning with a real talk.

**A Real World 'Pin Up & Return'**

Across the chapters of this book, when you think about it, I have demonstrated my planning and previewing (see Praise for *Real Talk?*) while putting the purpose of this book in context and pointing out evidence related to this book's purpose. This first edition of *Real Talk?* also demonstrates a real world pin up & return—this conclusion does not resolve a number of societal and school issues. Beyond the ongoing effects of

*Real Talk?*

COVID-19, schools across the United States of America are currently facing additional state and local factors of the reality imperative (see figure 1) which are all unresolved as I write the end of this book. As Tennessee's "Conference Committee Report on House Bill No. 580/Senate Bill No. 623" has signaled, it is likely that school educators across various states will find it challenging to discuss public issues like race, racism, and politics in the days ahead. This likelihood increases exponentially if the school educators who choose to have a real talk about public issues in their school are not supported by legislators, school board members, parents, community educators, college educators, education journalists, and other societal stakeholders. Although it is not impossible to have a real talk in American schools, even in states like Tennessee, I urge readers to expect difficulties to arise. But then again, excellent teaching and learning has never been easy to do, especially given the effects of public issues like race, racism, and politics on American schooling.

Regardless of all that remains unresolved in American society and our schools, there are countless reasons to be resolute. Here's one reason why I am resolute: the future I see for race, racism, and politics in the United States of America is the post-White future. In this post-White future, race would not be forgotten or feared. Rather, *White and Whiteness would be inconsequential.* Furthermore, in that post-White world, racism—if not eradicated—would be an undebated public and personal harm that is acted upon for elimination, like lead poisoning for instance. Moreover, the politics of that post-White world would be as messy as ever. Yet, the coalitions, contested flows of various capital—within and across post-White groups, and the power-brokers of that post-White system are difficult to imagine, even if we have some idea of the conflicts that post-White humanity would likely have. All of this stated differently, I am

## Real Talk?

resolute in 2021 because the post-White future that I see would become a reality through the same processes that have created our past and present: finite, accumulated thought and practice. As our present is not an inevitable repeat of our past, so our future is not an inevitable repeat of our present. We can *think and do* our way into such a [post-White future](), just as humans thought and did toward present day America and even toward the wider world that now is. All of this involves innumerable factors: large & small, far & near, singly, simultaneously, in sequence, extraordinary & ordinary, unknowable & well-known. Futures are (de)formed. What a remarkable reason for us to be resolute amid all that remains unresolved.

So, are you—are we—going to have a real talk?

# ABOUT THE AUTHOR

Marcus Croom is an Assistant Professor of Literacy, Culture, and Language Education in the School of Education and the Department of African American and African Diaspora Studies (AAADS) at Indiana University Bloomington. As an Executive Researcher at Brio Education Consulting, LLC, Croom uses research and experience to support the development of racial literacies in classrooms, schools, universities, businesses, organizations, and communities.

## Real Talk Protocol© Notes Template

| | |
|---|---|
| Plan | |
| Preview | |
| Put In Context | |
| Point Out Evidence | |
| Pin Up & Return | |

# Sources Included in *Real Talk?* Book

From the *Introduction* to the *Conclusion*
(scan QR Code below for this free pdf)

Made in the USA
Monee, IL
29 August 2023